Urine therapy
For Beginners
The Science Behind Urine Therapy, Bridging Ancient Wisdom with Modern Understanding.

Title:
Urine therapy
For Beginners

Subtitle
The Science Behind Urine Therapy, Bridging Ancient Wisdom with Modern Understanding.

Copyright © 2023 by (Tomasa Mayert)

All rights reserved. No part of this publication may be reproduced, distributed, or transmitted in any form or by any means, including photocopying, recording, or other electronic or mechanical methods, without the prior written permission of the publisher, except in the case of brief quotations embodied in critical reviews and certain other non-commercial uses permitted by copyright law. For permission requests, write to the publisher, addressed at the address below.

Printed in the United States of America.

ISBN: 9798870011332

TABLE OF CONTENT

INTRODUCTION 1

Welcome to the World of Urine Therapy .. 2

Understanding the Historical and Cultural Context 5

CHAPTER 1: THE BASICS OF URINE THERAPY 10

Definition and Origins 11

The Science Behind Urine Therapy 16

Myths and Misconceptions 22

CHAPTER 2: THE COMPONENTS OF URINE 28

Understanding the Composition 29

Nutrients and Substances Found in Urine 34

The Role of Hormones and Enzymes 39

CHAPTER 3: GETTING STARTED WITH URINE THERAPY 42

Collecting and Storing Urine 43

Choosing the Right Time and Conditions 47

Addressing Common Concerns 51

CHAPTER 4: HEALTH BENEFITS OF URINE THERAPY 57

Detoxification and Cleansing 58

Boosting the Immune System 61

Skin and Hair Care 64

Mental Clarity and Emotional Well-being 67

CHAPTER 5: INCORPORATING URINE THERAPY INTO YOUR DAILY ROUTINE 70

Oral Consumption 71

Topical Applications 74

External Uses and Compresses 76

Considerations for Incorporating Urine Therapy 78

CHAPTER 6: PRECAUTIONS AND CONSIDERATIONS......................... 81

Consultation with Healthcare Professionals 82

Potential Risks and Side Effects............ 86

Adjusting to the Practice Gradually 90

CHAPTER 7: FREQUENTLY ASKED QUESTIONS (FAQS)....................... 93

Common Concerns and Queries 94

Clarifying Doubts and Misconceptions ... 99

CHAPTER 8: BEYOND THE BASICS – ADVANCED PRACTICES................ 104

Exploring Variations in Urine Therapy.. 105

Combining with Other Holistic Approaches 110

CONCLUSION **115**

APPENDIX **117**

INTRODUCTION

Pee treatment, also known as urotherapy, is a method that includes making use of one's urine for a variety of objectives related to one's health and wellness. Throughout history, people have been fascinated and baffled by this topic. The purpose of this introductory chapter is to offer an overview of urine treatment by diving into its historical roots as well as its present significance. We can start to gain an appreciation for the deeply held beliefs and customs that have surrounded the practice of pee treatment for hundreds of years if we investigate the cultural and historical environment in which urine therapy has been practiced.

Welcome to the World of Urine Therapy

Welcome to the world of urine treatment, where ancient customs and contemporary curiosity collide. The idea of utilizing one's pee for medicinal purposes may initially appear unusual if not completely forbidden. Urine treatment has many facets, so it's important to approach the subject with an open mind and a willingness to learn about them as we begin this research.

The age-old practice of utilizing one's urine for therapeutic, cosmetic, or spiritual purposes is called urine treatment, often referred to as urotherapy or autourotherapy. The concept is based on the notion that urine, which is frequently written off as trash, really contains important nutrients, hormones, and other chemicals that might improve general health. Pee treatment has gained popularity due to its purported health advantages, even though it may seem unusual to those who are not familiar with it. Those looking for alternative ways to wellness have embraced urine therapy.

We must challenge stereotypes and approach urine treatment from a scientific perspective as we set out on this path. With material based on both historical traditions and current research, this book seeks to demystify the field. Knowing the basics of urine treatment will enable you to make well-informed judgments regarding your investigation and possible integration into your lifestyle, regardless of your level of skepticism or curiosity.

Understanding the Historical and Cultural Context

To comprehend the roots of urine therapy, one must delve into its historical and cultural context. Surprisingly, the use of urine for medicinal purposes dates back thousands of years and is deeply woven into the tapestry of diverse cultures worldwide. From ancient civilizations to traditional healing practices, urine has held a unique status as a substance with purported transformative properties.

- **Ancient Civilizations and Medical Traditions**

Urine treatment has a long history and dates back to ancient times when it was prized as a precious elixir with therapeutic qualities. For instance, the "Damar Tantra" and the "Shivambu Kalpa Vidhi," two ancient Indian writings, refer to the technique as "amaroli" or "shivambu." Urine's importance in cleaning the body and boosting general health is highlighted in these writings that discuss its usage for a variety of medical reasons.

Comparably, pee has long been utilized by traditional Chinese medicine practitioners as a diagnostic tool. They examine the color, odor, and other qualities of the urine to determine the health of the patient. Pee was used for medical purposes by the ancient Greeks and Romans as well, who acknowledged the potential therapeutic benefits of urine.

- **Urine Therapy in Different Cultures**

Urine treatment has been a component of many cultural traditions even outside of antiquity. Urine was utilized in purifying ceremonies and was thought to have mystical significance in some Native American societies. Urine is used in traditional medicine by indigenous societies throughout the globe because they consider it to be a powerful and natural ingredient.

Urine treatment is seen as part of a comprehensive approach to well-being in Ayurveda, the traditional medical system of India. The possible advantages of amaroli are discussed in Ayurvedic scriptures, which highlight its function in balancing doshas and promoting the body's inherent healing abilities.

Urine therapy's cultural and historical background is not without debate. Some civilizations have accepted it as a holy ritual, whereas others have written it off as superstition or pseudoscience. Urine therapy's many viewpoints and ideas may be understood to gain a more nuanced understanding of its historical significance as well as the elements that have led to its enduring popularity over the ages.

Urine treatment is still gaining popularity in the present day as interest in complementary and alternative medicine approaches to health expands. People are reconsidering the possible advantages of this age-old practice due to advances in scientific study and a resurgence of interest in traditional knowledge. We establish the foundation for a thorough knowledge that transcends the superficial opinions frequently connected to urine treatment by investigating the historical and cultural aspects of this technique.

CHAPTER 1: THE BASICS OF URINE THERAPY

A thorough investigation of urine therapy's foundational elements is necessary to comprehend it, from its definition and history to the underlying scientific theories. By addressing prevalent myths and misconceptions about urine treatment and providing insights into its scientific justification and historical background, this chapter seeks to demystify the fundamentals of the technique.

Definition and Origins

Pee treatment, at its heart, refers to the practice of utilizing one's urine for the aim of improving their overall health and fitness. This age-old technique may be traced back to several different civilizations and has been given some different names throughout history, including urotherapy, autourotherapy, and amaroli. Pee is a material that is traditionally regarded as waste by today's standards; nonetheless, the essential concept is to make use of the alleged therapeutic powers that may be found within urine.

- **Origins of Urine Therapy**

Urine treatment has its roots in ancient civilizations that existed thousands of years ago on several continents. The practice is known as "amaroli" or "shivambu" in ancient Indian scriptures such as the "Damar Tantra" and the "Shivambu Kalpa Vidhi." Pee is used for therapeutic and spiritual purposes, and these writings highlight the cleansing and rejuvenating properties of urine.

Urine has long been used as a diagnostic tool in traditional Chinese medicine. Practitioners evaluate a patient's health by examining their urine's color, odor, and other features. Urine's potential medicinal benefits were also recognized by the ancient Greeks and Romans, who used it in their medical procedures.

Urine treatment has ancient roots, but it is making a comeback because people are becoming more interested in holistic and alternative approaches to health. Urine treatment has been popular among those looking for alternative approaches to health and wellness. This practice is based on historical customs and the idea that the body has the natural capacity to cure itself.

- **_Defining Urine Therapy_**

Using, applying, or consuming one's pee for medical reasons is known as urine treatment. Urine is used in enemas and compresses, applied topically to the skin, and consumed as part of this therapy, among other approaches. Urine treatment proponents contend that the mixture of nutrients, hormones, enzymes, and other bioactive substances found in urine may have therapeutic benefits.

Urine treatment is a highly customized procedure; there is no one-size-fits-all method, and it is important to remember that. Urine treatment practitioners may follow different rituals and norms depending on cultural or personal preferences, and their methods and beliefs may differ as well.

Urine treatment is based on a comprehensive knowledge of the body and its linked processes, as we learn more about its foundational principles. Urine therapy's description and history serve as a starting point for investigating the scientific facets that support its possible advantages.

The Science Behind Urine Therapy

Understanding the scientific underpinnings of urine treatment is essential for anybody looking for a balanced viewpoint, even while the historical and cultural aspects of the practice provide insightful information as well. A scientific foundation for assessing the possible health advantages of urine treatment is provided by the physiological processes and urine composition.

- **Composition of Urine**

Water, electrolytes, metabolic waste products, hormones, and a variety of other chemicals make up the complex fluid known as urine. Urine is mostly made up of water (about 95 percent), with dissolved and suspended materials making up the final 5 percent. These consist of salts, enzymes, trace elements, urea, creatinine, and ammonia. Urine therapy proponents contend that this varied makeup adds to the treatment's possible benefits.

- **Urea and Nitrogenous Compounds**

One of the main ingredients in urine is urea, a nitrogenous substance that is created in the liver when proteins are broken down. It is eliminated by the kidneys, which is also what gives urine its distinct smell. Urea is a frequent element in skincare products and has been explored for its hydrating effects.

Supporters of urine treatment speculate that topically administered urea may have skin-nourishing properties.

- **Electrolytes and Minerals**

Urine includes necessary electrolytes and minerals, such as salt, potassium, calcium, and magnesium. Urine is excreted in the urine. These components play essential parts in preserving the fluid balance, as well as the function of the nerves and the muscles. Some proponents say that eating pee can help the body restore its supply of these essential elements, which will contribute to the individual's general health.

- **Hormones and Enzymes**

Additionally, urinalysis may detect minute quantities of hormones and enzymes. Melatonin, a hormone that is involved with sleep-wake cycles, has been discovered, for instance, in human urine. The presence of these bioactive molecules is hypothesized to affect a variety of physiological processes, including the maintenance of hormonal equilibrium and the control of sleep patterns, according to proponents of the theory.

- **Immune Factors**

White blood cells and antibodies, which are a part of the body's fight against pathogens, are immune system components found in urine. Urine treatment proponents speculate that these immunological components might be involved in the practice's possible immune-boosting benefits.

- **Scientific Studies and Research**

Pee includes a variety of substances that are known to have physiological purposes, however, it is important to emphasize that there has been little scientific study on urine treatment and that what is known is frequently anecdotal. There are few rigorous, peer-reviewed research that back up the many health claims made for urine treatment. The scientific community stresses that to properly demonstrate any health advantages associated with urine treatment, well-designed clinical studies are required.

- **Renal Function and Safety Considerations**

Pee therapy detractors frequently bring out possible hazards, especially about consuming urine. Re-ingesting waste materials might be harmful to one's health since the kidneys filter waste from the circulation to generate urine. Furthermore, unlike popular assumption, urine is not sterile and might include germs or other pollutants. These elements emphasize how crucial it is to proceed with caution and seek medical advice before beginning any kind of urine treatment.

Myths and Misconceptions

Urine treatment is shrouded in myths and misconceptions, as is the case with many alternative health therapies, which can engender both intrigue and mistrust. To acquire an educated opinion of the practice, it is necessary to distinguish reality from fantasy.

- **Myth: Urine Is Completely Sterile**

One widespread misunderstanding is that pee is completely sterile. Although the urine that emerges from the kidneys is largely devoid of germs, during urination it may pick up bacteria from the urethra and surrounding areas. Urine's supposed sterility is called into question and thus refutes the notion that it is essentially microorganism-free.

- **Myth: Urine Therapy Is a Cure-All**

The idea that urine treatment is a panacea for all ailments is another widespread misconception. Supporters could assert that it can cure anything from chronic ailments to skin conditions. But at the moment, there is insufficient scientific data to back up such generalized health claims. Urine treatment should be approached with reasonable expectations and an awareness that individual differences may exist in its results, if any.

- **Myth: Urine Therapy Is a Recent Trend**

Urine treatment is gaining popularity again, and while this may seem like a recent development, its origins are deep in historical and cultural customs. Urine treatment has a long history and has been used for millennia in many cultural contexts, which are sometimes overlooked by those who think it's a new fad.

- **Myth: All Urine Therapy Practices Are the Same**

Urine treatment is not a single, uniform approach; rather, it is a collection of techniques and viewpoints that may differ amongst practitioners. Urine consumption is a personal preference for some people, whereas external or topical treatments are preferred by others. The variety of methods emphasizes how crucial it is to understand that urine treatment is a highly customized procedure without a single, universally applicable technique.

- **Myth: Urine Therapy Is Backed by Overwhelming Scientific Evidence**

Pee treatment has several health benefits, however, there isn't much proof to back these claims despite some scientific investigation into the components of urine and their possible uses. Peer-reviewed, well-designed trials are required to fully establish the safety and efficacy of urine treatment.

- **Myth: Urine Therapy Is a Replacement for Conventional Medicine**

It is not appropriate to think of urine therapy as an alternative to traditional medical care. Urine therapy is a useful addition to some people's wellness regimens, but for the diagnosis and treatment of medical issues, it is important to see a healthcare provider. The technique needs to be seen in the larger framework of general health and well-being as an adjunctive or alternative strategy.

It is crucial to debunk prevalent misunderstandings, critically evaluate the scientific data, and approach urine therapy from a balanced standpoint while learning the fundamentals of the treatment. The upcoming chapters will include further practical details, health advantages, safety measures, and personal accounts, offering a thorough overview for anybody interested in urine treatment.

CHAPTER 2: THE COMPONENTS OF URINE

Urine is a complicated fluid that the kidneys create to remove waste items from the body. Understanding its composition is crucial to understanding the nuances of urine therapy. This chapter examines the several elements that makeup urine, such as nutrients, chemicals, hormones, and enzymes, illuminating the wide range of ingredients that go into its composition and their medicinal uses.

Understanding the Composition

Urine is composed of dissolved solutes, water, and waste products from the body's metabolic activities interacting dynamically. Detailed analysis of the constituent parts sheds light on the complex equilibrium that the kidneys preserve while filtering and excreting toxins.

- **Water: The Primary Constituent**

Urine is mostly composed of water; on average, this makes up around 95% of its volume. The principal job of the kidneys is to filter excess water and solutes from the circulation, which maintains the body's fluid balance and accounts for the high water content.

- **Electrolytes and Minerals**

Numerous minerals and electrolytes that are necessary for the body's correct operation may be found in urine. Electrolytes in urine include sodium, potassium, calcium, magnesium, chloride, and phosphate. These minerals are essential for the upkeep of nerve signals, muscular contraction, and cellular function.

- **Urea: Nitrogenous Waste Product**

One important nitrogenous waste product seen in urine is urea, which is created in the liver by breaking down proteins in a process called urea production. Urine's distinctive odor is caused by urea, which comprises a considerable amount of the solutes in the urine. Because of its moisturizing qualities, urea is included in several skincare products even though it is regarded as a waste product.

- **Creatinine: Metabolic Byproduct**

Another waste product that is produced when creatine phosphate in muscle tissue breaks down is creatinine, which is also present in urine. It acts as a kidney function indicator; high blood creatinine levels frequently indicate poor renal function. Creatinine is a helpful measure in clinical examinations of kidney health since the kidneys discharge it through urine.

Other Nitrogenous Compounds

Urine also contains additional nitrogenous substances including uric acid and ammonia in addition to urea and creatinine. To preserve the right physiological balance, these chemicals are eliminated through the urine and perform functions in the body's nitrogen metabolism.

- **Metabolic Waste Products**

Urine contains a variety of metabolic waste products that are a reflection of the body's continuous functions. These consist of residues from the metabolism of fatty acids, amino acids, and other molecules. Effective filters, the kidneys make sure that these waste products are removed from the body so that they don't build up in circulation.

- **Hormones and Enzymes**

Urine includes water and waste materials along with trace quantities of enzymes and hormones. These bioactive substances affect physiological functions and signaling pathways, playing a crucial role in the body's regulatory systems. Urine therapy has been shown to have health advantages, and the presence of hormones and enzymes in urine has sparked curiosity about their possible roles in the treatment.

Nutrients and Substances Found in Urine

Urine includes a variety of nutrients and chemicals that are necessary for body functioning in addition to waste products. Urine's total nutritional profile benefits from the presence of these chemicals, even if their quantities are comparatively modest when compared to food sources.

Vitamins

Water-soluble vitamins including vitamin C and B-complex vitamins can be found at trace levels in urine. These vitamins are essential for energy generation, immunological response, and cellular metabolism. The presence of vitamins contributes to the complexity of urine composition, even when the amounts are insufficient for nutritional reasons.

Minerals

Urine includes trace minerals such as zinc, copper, and selenium in addition to electrolytes like sodium and potassium. These minerals support several physiological functions, such as the action of enzymes, the immune system, and antioxidants. Pee's mineral composition is diverse, despite the comparatively low amounts. This is highlighted by the variety of minerals present in urine.

Amino Acids

Urine contains amino acids, which are the building blocks of proteins, as byproducts of the metabolism of proteins. Urine's low quantities of amino acids are indicative of the body's continuous turnover of proteins. Urine treatment proponents assert that urine may have some nutritional significance due to the presence of these amino acids.

Glucose

Normal conditions call for glucose to be absent from urine because the kidneys reabsorb it from the filtrate. Glycosuria, or the presence of glucose in the urine, is a defining feature of diseases such as diabetes mellitus, in which the kidneys are unable to adequately absorb high blood glucose levels. It is crucial to understand that the presence of glucose in urine may point to an underlying medical issue in the context of urine treatment.

Lactate and Ketones

Lactate and ketones may be present in urine, particularly under certain metabolic circumstances. Anaerobic metabolism produces lactate as a byproduct, whereas the breakdown of fatty acids produces ketones. Ketouria, or elevated amounts of ketones in the urine, can happen as a result of low-carb diets, fasting, or certain medical disorders.

Comprehending the existence of these substances in urine aids in a sophisticated analysis of its makeup.

The Role of Hormones and Enzymes

Urine contains trace levels of hormones and enzymes that are essential to the body's regulating systems. Urine treatment has gained attention because of the substances' possible functions in signaling pathways and enzymatic activities, even if their amounts in urine may not have a major effect on general health when eliminated.

Hormones

Hormones such as cortisol, adrenaline, and melatonin can be found in tiny levels in urine. Urine has been shown to contain melatonin, which is frequently connected to the sleep-wake cycle and may be involved in circadian rhythms. Urine also contains adrenaline, which is implicated in the "fight or flight" response, and cortisol, a stress hormone. Urine treatment proponents contend that these hormones may play a role in the practice's purported advantages, which include better sleep and less stress.

Enzymes

Urine is one of the physiological fluids that contain enzymes, which are biological catalysts that help in chemical processes in the body. Urine contains enzymes, although the amounts are not as high as in blood or tissues, but their existence still suggests metabolic activity. For instance, the presence of amylase in urine can be impacted by stress and food. Amylase is an enzyme involved in the metabolism and digestion of carbohydrates.

Investigating the various pathways via which urine treatment may work is made easier by having a solid understanding of the functions played by hormones and enzymes in urine. The amounts of hormones and enzymes in urine, however, could not be high enough to have a noticeable physiological impact, therefore it is important to approach these theories cautiously and with proof.

CHAPTER 3: GETTING STARTED WITH URINE THERAPY

When beginning the process of urine treatment, it is important to give serious thought to the various practical factors that are involved. This chapter offers detailed guidance for those who are interested in adding pee treatment into their health routines. Topics covered include the collection and storage of urine, as well as the selection of the appropriate time and circumstances for its application. In addition, frequent issues related to the practice are addressed, providing insights and comfort for those who are considering utilizing this traditional yet unorthodox method.

Collecting and Storing Urine

Urine collection and storage for therapeutic purposes necessitate a careful and sanitary procedure. Urine treatment practitioners may have personal preferences, but to guarantee the efficacy and safety of the urine collected, there are standard principles that may be adhered to.

- ***Hygiene and Cleanliness***

Make cleanliness and hygienic practices a top priority during the collecting procedure. Before gathering pee, wash your hands well and collect the urine in a sterile container. Steer clear of containers that might contaminate the urine or alter its makeup.

43

Tight-sealing lidded glass or BPA-free plastic containers are frequently advised.

- ***First Morning Urine***

The "midstream" pee, or first urine in the morning, is frequently chosen for treatment. It is thought that this urine is more concentrated and could have greater concentrations of certain chemicals. Let a tiny amount of the first morning's pee flow into the toilet and then guide the stream into the collection container.

- ***Midstream Collection***

To ensure that the sample is obtained from the middle of the stream, midstream urine collection requires letting the first portion of the urine run into the toilet. This technique is supposed to reduce the possibility of impurities coming from the external genitalia or urethra.

- **Urine for External Use**

You might require a different collection for compresses or topical treatments. In these situations, it is not necessary to consume the pee because it may be gathered in a sterile container and administered topically.

- **Storing Urine**

Urine should be stored out of direct sunlight in a dark, cold area after collection. While freezing is typically avoided because it may change the urine's content, refrigeration is still a possibility. Use glass containers with airtight lids if keeping for a long time to keep freshness and avoid evaporation.

Choosing the Right Time and Conditions

Many people believe that the timing of urine treatment and the settings under which it is performed are two of the most important elements in determining how successful it will be. Even though people have different tastes, there are certain common principles that practitioners might try to adhere to.

- **Morning Ritual**

The utilization of first-morning pee is emphasized in urine treatment, which is why many practitioners choose to include urine therapy in their daily practice. The greater concentration of certain chemicals that occurs during the first void of the day is commonly thought to be the cause of this phenomenon. The practice of beginning with a low dose and working up to a higher one, if and when desired, is a frequent technique for novices.

- **Empty Stomach**

Some people believe that if they drink their pee on an empty stomach, it will be easier for their bodies to absorb it, which might lead to increased health advantages. However, the level of personal comfort and the preferences of the individual are major factors in selecting the best time to consume urine.

- **Considerations for External Applications**

The timing could be looser for compresses or topical treatments. Urine used externally to treat skin issues like eczema or acne can be incorporated into a skincare regimen. Before applying urine, make sure the skin is clean, and keep an eye out for any negative responses.

- **Personalized Approach**

In the end, the ideal circumstances and timing for urine treatment are purely subjective and might differ from person to person. It's critical to pay attention to your body and modify the practice to suit your comfort level and lifestyle. The most important things in urine treatment are awareness and consistency, regardless of whether you decide to do it in the morning or at a time that suits you best.

Addressing Common Concerns

Despite its historical and cultural roots, urine treatment is not without its fair share of problems and misunderstandings. Providing clarity and easing apprehensions for persons who are considering or have recently begun urine treatment can be accomplished by addressing common concerns.

- *Hygiene and Safety*

The apparent lack of safety and cleanliness with urine treatment is one of the main worries. However, the danger of infection is reduced when appropriate hygiene precautions are taken, such as washing hands before collecting and using clean containers. The significance of maintaining cleanliness in the processes of collection, storage, and application cannot be overstated.

- *Taste and Odor*

Urine treatment proponents frequently identify the taste and odor of urine as major turnoffs. Even if supporters could contend that the flavor is light, it's important to recognize that everyone's taste buds are different. For individuals who are unfamiliar with the technique, experimenting with little sips and adding juice or other flavored liquids may help make the experience more enjoyable.

- *Nutrient Absorption and Redundancy*

Concerns have been raised by some people over the nutritional value of reingesting waste products. It is noteworthy that the body possesses strong regulatory systems to control the absorption and excretion of nutrients, and thus the concentrations of nutrients in urine are comparatively low. Urine treatment is also meant to support general wellness practices rather than take the place of a balanced diet.

- *Medical Conditions and Medications*

Before beginning urine treatment, people with pre-existing medical issues or those on medication should use caution and speak with healthcare providers. Urine treatment may not be appropriate for people with certain medical problems, such as diabetes or renal disease. Additionally, drugs may interact with urine constituents, making professional advice even more crucial.

- *Social Stigma and Acceptance*

For practitioners, the social stigma associated with urine treatment is a major problem. Since the procedure is unorthodox, some people can find it uncomfortable or skeptical. People must approach urine treatment with a feeling of privacy and autonomy, and make educated judgments about whether to reveal that they are participating in the practice.

- *Lack of Scientific Evidence*

Urine therapy's many health claims are supported by a small body of scientific data, which raises serious concerns. Urine treatment is associated with a wide range of health advantages; however, there is a dearth of rigorous, peer-reviewed research that validates the numerous substances found in urine that have physiological roles that are recognized. Practitioners need to approach the profession with a realistic awareness of the status of science as it stands right now.

Urine treatment is a personal choice, and people should feel empowered to make decisions that are in line with their comfort levels, beliefs, and health considerations. This is crucial to stress while addressing these issues. A careful and knowledgeable approach to urine treatment must include consulting medical specialists and maintaining bodily awareness.

CHAPTER 4: HEALTH BENEFITS OF URINE THERAPY

Beyond its historical and cultural settings, the research of urine treatment has expanded to include the possible health advantages that are attributed to this age-old practice. This chapter dives into important areas where proponents of urine therapy say that the treatment may give good results. These areas include detoxification and cleaning, strengthening the immune system, skin and hair care, and enhancing mental clarity and emotional well-being.

Detoxification and Cleansing

There are a lot of different claims that can be made about urine treatment, but one of the most important ones is that it can detoxify and purify. Urine is said to include components, such as urea and other waste products, that can assist in the body's natural process of eliminating toxins, according to proponents of the theory.

- **Urea as a Detoxifying Agent**

Urine's main ingredient, urea, is frequently mentioned as a possible detoxifier. Ammonia is a byproduct of protein metabolism that the liver transforms into urea, which is then eliminated through urine. Proponents suggest that urea could aid in the body's natural detoxification processes by aiding in the elimination of nitrogenous waste and other pollutants.

- **Hydration and Kidney Function**

Urine treatment proponents stress the need to stay hydrated throughout detoxification. Urine is how the kidneys filter and remove waste items from the circulation, hence it is crucial to drink enough water to sustain kidney function. People can help their kidneys remove pollutants more effectively by drinking plenty of water.

- **Considerations for Detoxification Practices**

Urine treatment as a means of detoxifying is a fascinating notion, but it must be approached cautiously. The body contains complex systems for breaking down and getting rid of toxins, mostly through the kidneys and liver. It is usually advised to take a comprehensive approach to detoxification, which involves maintaining a healthy lifestyle, eating balanced food, and drinking enough water. Urine therapy users who are thinking about using it for detoxification should speak with medical specialists to be sure the procedure will help them achieve their overall health objectives.

Boosting the Immune System

The possibility of urine treatment to strengthen the immune system is another stated advantage. White blood cells and antibodies are two examples of the several substances found in urine that help the body fight against diseases. Urine treatment proponents contend that adopting this practice into daily life may improve immune function.

- ***Immune Factors in Urine***

White blood cells, antibodies, and other immunological components that are a part of the body's defensive processes can be found in urine. Urine may deliver these immunological components into the body through consumption or application, according to proponents, enhancing the immune response.

- **Potential Mechanisms**

It is unclear how urine treatment could affect the immune system through various methods. According to some hypotheses, the body's capacity to identify and fight diseases may be improved if modest quantities of immune components are introduced because they may cause an immune response.

- ***Balancing the Immune System***

Urine treatment proponents emphasize how it may strengthen the immune system, but it's important to understand how the immune system is delicately balanced. Autoimmune disorders can be brought on by excessive stimulation or improper immune reactions. Urine treatment should be used cautiously and after consulting with medical specialists by those with pre-existing immunological problems or those using immunosuppressive medicines.

Skin and Hair Care

Urine therapy has a long tradition of being connected with the treatment of skin and hair conditions. Some people believe that the components of urine, such as urea and minerals, may have positive benefits on the skin and hair if they are applied topically.

- ***Urea for Skin Moisture***

Natural humectant urea is well-known for its moisturizing qualities. It helps keep skin hydrated and is frequently used in skincare products. Urine used topically, according to proponents, may help hydrate the skin and treat ailments including eczema and dry skin.

- **Minerals and Nutrients for Hair**

Urine contains a variety of minerals and nutrients, which has led to the speculation that drinking it could be beneficial to one's hair health. Some proponents argue that putting urine on the scalp might deliver nutrients that help the growth of healthy hair and the overall vitality of the scalp.

- **External Uses of Urine**

Urine can be used topically on the skin and hair for a variety of purposes, including washing the face, acting as a moisturizer, or rinsing the hair. Even if there have been reports of these methods being beneficial for certain people, it is essential to take into account the various types of skin and how they react. It is suggested to do patch testing to evaluate any potential adverse responses.

Mental Clarity and Emotional Well-being

Proponents of urine treatment also claim that the practice is associated with mental clarity and emotional well-being. The relationship between urine treatment and mental health is complex, comprising not only the physiological but also the psychological components of the patient.

- **Hormones and Neurotransmitters**

Hormones and neurotransmitters, including melatonin and serotonin, can be found in trace levels in urine. These substances are essential for controlling mood and sleep cycles. The administration of these drugs through urine treatment, according to proponents, may improve mental health.

- **Psychological Factors**

Urine treatment has the potential to be psychologically beneficial for certain people. The routines and rituals connected to self-care activities can benefit mental health. Using alternative health techniques may provide one with a feeling of empowerment and control, which can help foster a good outlook.

- **Considerations for Mental Health Practices**

Urine treatment may not be directly associated with improved mental health, but the mind-body relationship is a multifaceted and personalized element of well-being. The promotion of a positive outlook via practices like self-care, mindfulness, and healthy habits can enhance general well-being. Urine treatment, like any other alternative health practice, requires people to approach it mindful of their mental health issues and seek professional assistance as needed.

CHAPTER 5: INCORPORATING URINE THERAPY INTO YOUR DAILY ROUTINE

Those who are interested in the age-old practice of urine treatment will find that incorporating it into their routine requires careful study and a specialized strategy. This chapter examines a variety of ways in which urine treatment may be incorporated into daily life, such as oral ingestion, topical applications, and external usage using compresses.

Oral Consumption

Starting Small:

It's standard advice for anyone thinking about consuming pee orally to start a little. If you choose to proceed, start with a few drops or a teaspoon and progressively increase the amount. People may evaluate their comfort level with the practice and adjust to the taste with this progressive method.

Choosing the Right Time:

Urination is preferred by many practitioners to be consumed in the morning, usually with the first urine of the day. The theory is that following a night's sleep, the urine is more concentrated and could contain larger concentrations of certain chemicals. The ideal moment for oral ingestion is arbitrary, though, and people are free to select a time that suits their schedule and tastes.

Mixing with Other Beverages:

Some people combine urine with other drinks, including water or juice, to improve the flavor. Those who are unfamiliar with the practice or find the taste difficult may find this very beneficial. People might discover a combination that appeals to them by experimenting with various mixes.

Frequency and Consistency:

Different practitioners may consume differently regularly. While some may want to use urine treatment every day, others may only do so sometimes. Maintaining consistency is essential, and people should evaluate how the practice affects them over time. A key component of integrating urine treatment into a routine is paying attention to the body and making modifications depending on individual experiences.

Topical Applications

Facial Cleansing:

Urine is used to cleanse the face while doing topical treatments like scrubbing the face. Urine, according to some practitioners, may gently cleanse the skin and improve its health. This is frequently done as part of a skincare regimen or first thing in the morning.

Moisturizing and Nourishing the Skin:

Some people think that pee, especially the first urine of the morning, has moisturizing qualities since it contains urea. Some people include applying urine to their skin as a moisturizer in their everyday skincare procedures. It is advised to properly cleanse the skin before use.

Hair Rinse:

Another topical use is rinsing urine through your hair. Urine's nutrients and minerals are said to encourage healthy hair by supporters. As the last stage in their hair care regimen, some people decide to rinse their hair with urine after washing it with conventional shampoo.

External Uses and Compresses

Wound Healing and First Aid:

Urine treatment can be used externally for wound healing and first aid. Urine used topically for small burns, scrapes, and wounds is said by some practitioners to aid in recovery. Urine's ability to remain sterile after exiting the body is frequently mentioned as one of its possible uses in first aid.

Compresses for Muscles and Joints:

Another technique of external administration is urine compresses. This is putting urine-soaked cloths or bandages on achy muscles or joints. Some believe comfort comes from the warmth of the compress and the urine's supposed healing qualities.

Eye Drops for Eye Health:

Urine mixed with water has been used traditionally as eye drops in several cultures, albeit this practice needs careful thought and advice from medical experts. The theory is that the solution might promote eye health and aid in cleaning the eyes. On the other hand, care and expert advice should be sought for any application close to delicate regions, such as the eyes.

Considerations for Incorporating Urine Therapy

Individualized Approach:

Urine treatment integration into a daily regimen is a very customized procedure. The practice should be tailored to the comfort level, preferences, and health needs of each individual. The significance of a customized strategy is underscored by the possibility that what suits one person may not be appropriate for another.

Health Considerations:

Before introducing urine treatment into their routines, those with pre-existing medical disorders, such as diabetes or renal disease, or those on medication, should use caution and speak with healthcare specialists. Prioritizing general health and well-being is essential, as is getting expert help when necessary.

Mindful Engagement:

It's crucial to approach urine treatment mindfully. A mindful approach to urine treatment involves being aware of one's body, noting any physical or emotional reactions, and modifying the practice accordingly. Practitioners have to be willing to try out various techniques to establish a regimen that fits their objectives and way of life.

Respecting Personal Boundaries:

Urine treatment is a private profession; people are free to discuss their experiences with others or to keep them secret. Urine treatment must be integrated into daily life while honoring personal limits and making decisions that fit one's comfort zone.

CHAPTER 6: PRECAUTIONS AND CONSIDERATIONS

Urine treatment has been around for quite some time and is used by some people; nonetheless, it is essential to approach it with great deliberation and to be aware of the possible hazards involved. This chapter examines some of the most important precautions and concerns, highlighting how important it is to speak with qualified medical specialists, gain an awareness of the potential dangers and adverse effects, and work up to the practice gradually.

Consultation with Healthcare Professionals

Personal Health Evaluation

It is important to speak with medical specialists before starting urine treatment. This is particularly important for people who already have health issues, such as diabetes, renal illness, or autoimmune disorders. Individual health evaluations can be performed by medical experts who consider the patient's general health state, current medicines, and medical history.

Assessment of Kidney Function

Since the kidneys generate urine, evaluating renal function is an essential part of the consultation. People who have impaired kidney function may be more vulnerable to electrolyte abnormalities and other side effects from urine treatment. Tests for kidney function can be carried out by medical practitioners to assess how well the kidneys filter and eliminate waste.

Handling Diabetes

Urine treatment presents new issues for those with diabetes. Glycosuria, or the presence of glucose in the urine, is a sign of uncontrolled diabetes. For people with diabetes to successfully manage their disease and make sure that urine treatment does not affect blood glucose levels, speaking with healthcare experts is vital.

Drug Interactions

Urine's constituent parts can interact with some drugs, perhaps compromising their safety or effectiveness. Patients using medication for different ailments should let their medical providers know if they plan to participate in urine treatment. This makes it possible to thoroughly assess any possible interactions and change prescriptions as necessary.

Total Health Evaluation

Beyond particular medical issues, a comprehensive evaluation of general health is essential. Healthcare experts can offer advice on whether urine treatment fits a person's health objectives and whether adjustments or safety measures are required.

Potential Risks and Side Effects

Unbalanced Electrolytes

The possibility of an imbalance in electrolytes is one of the main issues with urine therapy. Salt and potassium are examples of electrolytes that are vital for many physiological processes, such as nerve and muscle contraction. Large urine intakes without taking the needs of the individual in mind can cause imbalances and increase the risk of dehydration or hyperkalemia.

Renal Strain

When it comes to removing waste from the body, the kidneys are crucial. Without taking the necessary safety precautions, urine therapy can put undue strain on the kidneys, especially in those who already have renal disease. Serious health problems could arise from kidney strain, which can also impair kidney function.

Hazard of Infection

Though contamination can happen during collection and storage, urine is normally sterile when it leaves the body. Urinary tract infections may become more likely if bacteria are introduced into the system through the use of dirty containers or poor hygiene during the collection process (UTIs). Urine therapy participants should put hygiene first to reduce their risk of infection.

Responses to Allergies

Using urine topically or externally can increase the risk of allergic reactions, especially in people with sensitive skin. To determine any possible negative reactions, patch testing is advised before broad application. People who have a history of allergies or sensitive skin should use caution when using this product and stop using it if they become irritated.

Effects on the Mind

Participating in complementary and alternative medicine, such as urine therapy, may have psychological effects. People should be aware of their mental health and the potential effects the practice may have on their general outlook. There may be uncomfortable, anxious, or guilty feelings; it's important to deal with these feelings through introspection or expert assistance.

Adjusting to the Practice Gradually

Begin small and keep an eye on it

Those who are interested in urine treatment are recommended to start gently and evaluate their results to reduce potential hazards and negative effects. Starting with tiny doses enables people to assess their comfort level and see any physical or emotional effects, whether through oral ingestion or topical treatments.

Gradual Elevation

If the patient decides to proceed with urine treatment, a progressive increase in dosage might be taken into consideration. With this method, the body may gradually become used to the practice. It's critical to continue monitoring health status changes and modify practice as necessary.

Frequent Check-ins for Health

Individuals undergoing urine treatment must see medical specialists for regular check-ups. Responsibly taking care of oneself requires keeping an eye on general health, renal function, and any changes in medical issues. Maintaining open lines of communication with medical experts guarantees that practice modifications are in line with patient demands.

Paying Attention to the Body

When undergoing urine treatment, people should pay attention to the body's essential input. When discomfort, unfavorable responses, or changes in health status arise, it's important to reevaluate the procedure and, if required, consult medical specialists for advice.

CHAPTER 7: FREQUENTLY ASKED QUESTIONS (FAQS)

Like any non-traditional technique, urine therapy raises several queries and worries. This chapter answers frequently asked questions, clears up myths, and offers guidance to assist people in understanding and navigating the world of urine treatment.

Common Concerns and Queries

Q1: Is the use of urine treatment safe?

A1: In every health profession, safety is of utmost importance. Urine treatment is usually regarded as safe for certain people when used appropriately and with good cleanliness. Nonetheless, some groups may be more vulnerable than others, such as individuals with diabetes or renal diseases. It is crucial to speak with medical specialists to evaluate each person's health situation and decide whether urine treatment is appropriate.

Q2: Is there a flavor associated with urine therapy?

A2: Urine's flavor is subjective and might differ from person to person. Some people find it moderate, while others may find it salty or somewhat harsh. Individuals who are new to urine treatment sometimes begin with lower doses and may discover that the taste becomes better with time. Trying out various techniques, including diluting urine with juice or water, might help make the process more bearable.

Q3: Can urine therapy cure diseases?

A3: Urine treatment has been linked to several health advantages by certain practitioners, but there isn't enough data to back claims that it may treat particular conditions. The method shouldn't be thought of as a substitute for traditional medical care. Rather, it is frequently regarded as an alternate or complementary strategy in the larger framework of holistic well-being. Medical specialists should be consulted by people with diseases to receive the proper diagnosis and treatment.

Q4: What is the impact of urine treatment on hydration?

A4: Water makes up the majority of the urine, thus drinking it can help you stay hydrated overall. It's crucial to remember that there might be variations in the solute content in urine. Urine treatment should not be the only source of fluid intake; drinking water is still a crucial part of staying hydrated. It's advised to stick to a balanced and diverse hydration regimen that includes water and other liquids.

Q5: Can nutritional deficits result from urine therapy?

A5: The body has strong regulatory systems for nutrient absorption and excretion, so even while urine includes trace levels of nutrients, the concentrations are generally low. When people eat a healthy, balanced diet, using urine treatment as a supplemental approach is unlikely to result in nutritional deficits. It shouldn't, however, take the place of necessary dietary sources of vitamins and minerals.

Clarifying Doubts and Misconceptions

Q6: Is there scientific evidence to promote urine therapy?

A6: There is little scientific proof to back up the many health claims made for urine treatment. Urine treatment is associated with several substances that have physiologically recognized uses, but there isn't much well-designed, peer-reviewed research on the whole range of health advantages. Advocates frequently use historical viewpoints and anecdotal evidence. Urine treatment proponents ought to approach the procedure with a realistic grasp of the state of science as it stands right now.

Q7: Is the body detoxified by urine therapy?

A7: There is disagreement over the idea of using urine treatment for detoxification. Urine does contain waste materials and metabolic wastes, but the body has complex systems in place to filter and get rid of toxins, mostly through the kidneys and liver. Urine treatment should only be used sparingly; instead, people are advised to approach detoxification holistically, with a healthy lifestyle and balanced food.

Q8: Is urine therapy a treatment for skin diseases?

A8: Urine treatment proponents assert that topical use of urea may help the skin by providing hydrating characteristics to the skin. Some people say they've had success treating skin issues including acne and eczema. Urine treatment is useful for treating skin disorders, however, the outcomes might differ greatly depending on the patient. It is advised to conduct a patch test to determine skin sensitivity before broad application.

Q9: When is the best time to use urine therapy?

A9: When using urine treatment topically or orally, the best time to administer it is frequently arbitrary. Pee treatment is frequently incorporated into morning routines, with a focus on using first-morning urine by practitioners. Individual differences exist in the optimal time, though, and lifestyle factors and personal preferences are important factors to take into account. For individuals who are implementing urine treatment into their routines, consistency in the selected time and manner is essential.

Q10: Can urine treatment take the place of prescription drugs?

A10: Urine therapy is not intended to replace traditional forms of medical care and should not be treated as such. Even though some people may choose to include urine therapy as part of their overall wellness routines, it is essential to seek the advice and treatment of qualified medical specialists when attempting to diagnose or treat any medical ailment.

Within the larger framework of one's health and well-being as a whole, the practice needs to be seen as a complementary or alternative strategy.

CHAPTER 8: BEYOND THE BASICS – ADVANCED PRACTICES

As people grow more familiar with urine treatment, there is a possibility that they will decide to investigate more sophisticated methods and variants. This chapter delves into the intricacies of advanced urine therapy, including the exploration of variations in the practice and the combination of it with other holistic approaches for a more comprehensive wellness journey. Specifically, this chapter focuses on the benefits of combining advanced urine therapy with other holistic approaches.

Exploring Variations in Urine Therapy

Q1: Is there more than one way to practice urine therapy?

Answer: Urine therapy is not a treatment that works for everyone. In addition to the standard procedures of topical treatments and oral absorption, there are other options that people might investigate according to their comfort zones and particular tastes.

- **Urine Fasting**

Urine treatment is approached more intensively during a urine fast. For a set amount of time, some practitioners decide to solely drink their pee, often with juice and/or water. Urine fasting has many justifications;

some people believe it has spiritual or cleansing properties. Urine fasting, however, should be carefully considered, and speaking with medical authorities is advised.

- **Urine Massage and Therapy**

The process of putting urine directly into the skin and rubbing it in is known as urine massage. Supporters assert that this technique may improve the skin's ability to absorb nutrients and support general skin health. Urine treatment may also be added to holistic massage techniques, although doing so calls for a thorough evaluation of each client's preferences as well as ethical issues.

- **Urine Enemas**

Urine enemas are medical procedures in which urine is therapeutically introduced into the rectum. Some people think that using this technique might aid in intestinal health and cleansing. To guarantee safety and suitability for certain medical situations, this method should be used with caution and after consulting with medical experts.

- **Urine Eye Drops**

In the past, certain civilizations have utilized diluted urine as eye drops. Advocates contend that this exercise might promote eye health and aid in cleaning the eyes. On the other hand, care and expert advice should be sought for any application close to delicate regions, such as the eyes.

- **Nasal Irrigation with Urine**

Nasal irrigation involves flushing the nasal passages with a saline solution. Some individuals explore the practice of nasal irrigation with diluted urine, associating it with potential respiratory and sinus benefits. As with any advanced practice, consultation with healthcare professionals is advisable to ensure safety and appropriateness.

Q2: Can these variations be combined?

Answer: Urine treatment variants come in a multitude of combinations, and practitioners are free to experiment with different approaches according to their tastes and wellness objectives. It is advisable for individuals to use caution and attention when engaging in advanced techniques, and to seek expert supervision when necessary.

Combining with Other Holistic Approaches

- **Ayurveda and Urine Therapy**

The ancient Indian medical system known as Ayurveda places a strong emphasis on maintaining the balance of physiological energy and overall well-being. Urine treatment can be included in daily routines by some Ayurvedic practitioners, who will do so following Ayurvedic principles for a comprehensive approach to health.

- **Yoga and Urine Therapy**

Yoga is a complete discipline that includes breathing exercises, meditation, and physical postures. Urine treatment is something that some yoga practitioners use in their overall wellness regimen. The individualized method of urine treatment is complemented by the thoughtful and comprehensive practice of yoga, which is in line with the ideals of self-awareness and balance.

- **Meditation and Mindfulness**

The main goals of mindfulness and meditation are to develop mental clarity and present-moment awareness. Urine therapy is something that some people believe improves their general well-being when they incorporate it into their mindfulness or meditation practices. Urine therapy is a mindful practice that embodies the concepts of bodily awareness and present-moment awareness.

- **Herbalism and Natural Medicine**

Herbalism and natural medicine are occasionally investigated in combination with urine treatment. As part of a complete approach to holistic health, people may choose to combine urine treatment with the usage of vitamins, herbs, or other natural medicines. Urine treatment and herbalism must be integrated with careful consideration for each patient's unique medical situation and any interactions.

- **Holistic Detoxification Practices**

The goal of holistic detoxification techniques is to assist the body's inherent capacity to get rid of pollutants. Urine treatment can be used by some people in more comprehensive detoxification regimens that also include other detox techniques, herbal supplements, and dietary adjustments. Detoxification procedures must be approached sensibly and after consulting medical experts.

Q3: Can urine therapy be part of a comprehensive holistic approach?

Answer: Urine treatment does fit into a whole, holistic approach to well-being, yes. Urine treatment may be used in conjunction with other holistic therapies when it is carefully incorporated and tailored to each patient's unique health needs. On the other hand, people ought to put their general health and well-being first and base their judgments on their particular situation.

CONCLUSION

In summing up, this beginner's guide has provided an in-depth exploration of the field of urine treatment. The complex nature of this age-old activity has been examined from a variety of perspectives, ranging from historical backgrounds to practical factors. Urine treatment is a terrain that individuals must learn to navigate, and the key to doing so successfully comes in approaching it with an open mind, a critical viewpoint, and a dedication to conscious involvement. On the way to achieving holistic well-being, the guide encourages individuals to proceed with their investigations and helps to cultivate an ongoing conversation that integrates historical knowledge, contemporary perspectives, and personal experiences.

APPENDIX

Individuals who are interested in investigating urine treatment beyond its essential characteristics might use the information contained in this appendix as a useful resource. In this section, we will investigate a variety of urine treatment applications that may be made at home using recipes and do-it-yourself (DIY) techniques. It is essential to approach these applications with an open mind, realizing that an individual's specific tastes and comfort levels have a considerable impact on the degree to which they participate in urine treatment.

Recipes for Oral Consumption:

1. Morning Elixir:

Ingredients:

- One portion of morning pee, taken midstream.
- One part is herbal tea or water (optional for dilution).
- One tsp honey or other natural sweetener (optional for flavor).

Instructions:

- In the morning, gather the urine in midstream.
- If preferred, dilute the urine with an equivalent amount of water or herbal tea.
- For taste, you can add honey or your favorite natural sweetener.

- Stir well and drink on an empty stomach.

2. Citrus Infusion:

Ingredients:

- One portion of fresh urine in midstream.
- two parts citrus juice, freshly squeezed (e.g., orange, lemon).
- Cubes of ice (optional).

Instructions:

- Gather the pee in midstream.
- Add freshly squeezed lemon juice to the urine.
- If you would want your beverage cold, add some ice cubes.
- Mix well and eat.

3. Herbal Blend:

Ingredients:

- One portion of fresh urine in midstream.
- one-part infusion of herbs (e.g., chamomile, peppermint).
- Ginger slices or a small amount of cinnamon (optional).

Instructions:

- Gather the pee in midstream.
- Steeping plants in hot water yields a prepared herbal infusion.
- Combine the herbal infusion with the urine.
- If desired, garnish with sliced ginger or a dash of cinnamon for extra taste.
- Mix and savor.

DIY Topical Applications:

1. Facial Toner:

Ingredients:

- 1 part distilled water.
- 1 part fresh, midstream urine.
- Cotton pads.

Instructions:

- Gather the pee in midstream.
- Add the same amount of distilled water to the urine to dilute it.
- Dip a cotton pad into the concoction.
- Avoid getting too close to the eyes while applying the toner.
- You may pat it gently with a fresh towel or let it air dry.

2. Hair Rinse:

Ingredients:

- One portion of fresh urine in midstream.
- Two portions of water.
- Fragrance using essential oils (such as lavender or tea tree) (optional).

Instructions:

- Gather the pee in midstream.
- Use two parts of water to dilute the pee.
- If you would like, add a few drops of essential oil for aroma.
- Use the combination as a last rinse for your hair after shampooing.
- After letting it sit for a minute, give it a good water rinse.

3. Skin Moisturizer:

Ingredients:

- 1 part fresh midstream urine.
- 1 part aloe vera gel/coconut oil.
- Essential oil of lavender for scent (optional).

Instructions:

- Collect the urine from the midstream.
- Combine equal parts pee with aloe vera gel or melted coconut oil.
- For scent, add a few drops of lavender essential oil.
- Blend thoroughly and apply to clean, dry skin as a moisturizer.

DIY External Uses and Compresses:

1. Wound Cleansing Compress:

Ingredients:

- Cotton pad or sterile gauze.
- 1 part fresh midstream urine.

Instructions:

- Collect the urine from the midstream.
- Soak a sterile gauze pad or cotton pad with urine.
- Carefully apply the compress to the wound.
- Leave it for a short period and replace it as needed.
- Collect the pee from the stream's center.

- Soak the sterile gauze or cotton pad in the urine.
- Apply the compress to the wound carefully.
- After a short period, replace it.

2. Joint Pain Relief Compress:

Ingredients:

- Use a clean cloth or bandage.
- 1 part fresh midstream urine.

Instructions:

- Collect the urine from the midstream.
- Soak the bandage or cloth in the urine.
- Place the compress over the afflicted joint.

- Leave it in place for a few minutes, adjusting as needed.

3. Eye Compress:

Ingredients:

- A cotton ball that has been sterilized.
- 1 part midstream fresh urine (diluted with an equal part of water).

Instructions:

- Collect the urine from the midstream.
- Dilute the urine with the same amount of water.
- Soak a clean cotton ball with diluted urine.
- Place the cotton ball gently on closed eyelids for a calming compress.

Important Considerations:

- Hygiene: To avoid contamination, keep your hands and urine-collecting containers clean.

- Allergic Responses: Before widespread usage, patch test topical treatments on a small area of skin to look for any adverse reactions.

- Diluting urine with water or other drinks might make the experience more bearable for people new to urine treatment.

- Individual Variation: Personal tastes are important; try different recipes to find what works best for you.

It's critical to approach these recipes and applications with a sense of individual comfort and preferences in mind. Consultation with healthcare experts is recommended, as with any health practice, especially for persons with pre-existing medical issues or concerns. These DIY uses are provided as recommendations, and people should use their discretion and judgment when incorporating them into their lives. routines.

Made in the USA
Columbia, SC
04 June 2025